HOW TO KNOW IF HE REALLY LOVES YOU

KINGSLEY OKONKWO

Published and Printed in Nigeria by:

MillionValues Concepts,
105, Igi-Olugbin, Pedro Road, Lagos
Tel: 08185710897 | millionvalues@gmail.com

Cover: DesignsbyFemmy

To contact the author:
Tel: 08077714411, 08077714413

CONTENTS

DEDICATION

To all the women who desire to understand the true meaning of love as well as avoid unpleasant experiences so that they can be better guided in the choice of a life partner and ultimately have the marriage of their dreams.

INTRODUCTION

No one wants to spend their lives with someone who doesn't love them. And this makes absolute sense. Why on earth would you want to be in a relationship with or plan to get married to someone who you are not absolutely sure you love or loves you in return? Love is the very essence of relationships and marriages. As a matter of fact, one of the most common questions I get asked during counselling sessions is, "Pastor, how do I know if a person truly loves me?" And it is so important to ask this question because a lot of single people actually think what they have for each other is love. Love, unfortunately, is one of the most misunderstood, misconstrued and misrepresented words in our world today.

In a relationship, it is easy to hear people say, "I love you." But after they get married, they realize they never truly loved each other. Every couple that is divorced today thought at some point that they loved their spouse. At some point they felt, "I love this man or woman" but later, it became, "I hate this man or woman." So, you actually need to be able to know if what you are feeling is love because not every feeling you have is love. A lot of single people are not so knowledgeable in this regard, so they assume every feeling they have is love.

A young lady might meet a nice-looking

man for the first time and because she loses her composure around him and can't seem to forget him, she assumes it is love. No, that's not love. You need to understand that there are many other emotions that feel or look like love but they are not love. Just because you are always thinking about a man or woman does not mean you love them. In fact, some of those feelings are just infatuation or obsession or sexual attraction. You will eventually have such feelings for many other people as you go through life but it is not necessarily always love.

2 Samuel 13:1-17(NIV) tells a very remarkable story to buttress this;

In the course of time, Amnon son of David fell in love with Tamar, the beautiful sister of Absalom son of David.

Amnon became so obsessed with his sister Tamar that he made himself ill. She was a virgin, and it seemed impossible for him to do anything to her.

In our time, we would say, no doubt what Amnon had for Tamar was true love. He couldn't eat, he was growing thin, in fact he was sick; love sick. I also see single people go through the same thing these days. You'll hear them say things like, "When I see him or her, I can't breathe..." Immediately, I tell them, "That's not love, that is an asthma attack, go and get an inhaler."

Amnon, also, was so obsessed with his half-sister Tamar, that he made himself sick. Let's read on,

Now Amnon had an adviser named Jonadab son of Shimeah, David's

brother. Jonadab was a very shrewd man.

Please note this, one of the biggest lessons you can learn from this is that as a single person, you cannot successfully fail without bad friends or bad advice. That is why getting the right knowledge about relationships and surrounding yourself with the right people is key.

He asked Amnon, "Why do you, the king's son, look so haggard morning after morning? Won't you tell me?" Amnon said to him, "I'm in love with Tamar, my brother Absalom's sister."

"Go to bed and pretend to be ill," Jonadab said. "When your father comes to see you, say to him, 'I would like my sister Tamar to come and give me something to eat. Let

her prepare the food in my sight so I may watch her and then eat it from her hand.'"

So Amnon lay down and pretended to be ill. When the king came to see him, Amnon said to him, "I would like my sister Tamar to come and make some special bread in my sight, so I may eat from her hand."

David sent word to Tamar at the palace: "Go to the house of your brother Amnon and prepare some food for him." So Tamar went to the house of her brother Amnon, who was lying down. She took some dough, kneaded it, made the bread in his sight and baked it. Then she took the pan and served him the bread, but he refused to eat.

"Send everyone out of here," Amnon said. So everyone left him. Then

Amnon said to Tamar, "Bring the food here into my bedroom so I may eat from your hand." And Tamar took the bread she had prepared and brought it to her brother Amnon in his bedroom. But when she took it to him to eat, he grabbed her and said, "Come to bed with me, my sister."

"No, my brother!" she said to him. "Don't force me! Such a thing should not be done in Israel! Don't do this wicked thing. What about me? Where could I get rid of my disgrace? And what about you? You would be like one of the wicked fools in Israel. Please speak to the king; he will not keep me from being married to you." But he refused to listen to her, and since he was stronger than she, he raped her.

Then Amnon hated her with intense

hatred. In fact, he hated her more than he had loved her. Amnon said to her, "Get up and get out!"

This is such a sad story because this is still the reality for some people, even today, which is why I believe everyone must learn about relationships. Take a closer look at what happened here. Prior to this, Amnon thought he was in love with Tamar; he couldn't eat, couldn't sleep, he was sick and everyone around saw how much it was affecting him too. It wasn't a prank, he wasn't faking it, but the problem was not love, maybe infatuation, maybe lust, maybe just sexual passion but it was definitely not love. So, if you notice, once he got what he wanted everything changed. Single ladies you can take a lesson from this, you need to understand this, when a man sleeps with you, the way he sees you changes. Before he sleeps with you, he feels like he can't live without you, he's thinking of you constantly, he's calling you every time but once he sleeps with you everything changes. He also can't explain what is happening; he doesn't understand why all of a sudden, he can't stand you, he cannot place his fingers on why he hates you so much, but he just does. Sadly, some people experience this shift in marriage.

A lot of people, like Amnon, also think what they have for one another is love and because of this they rush into marriage only to discover it has nothing to do with love but by that time, they are already married with children. And that is why God tells single people to keep sex out of their relationships. Sex confuses issues and that's the problem. So, keeping sex out of your relationship is one of the quickest ways to know the person that truly loves you.

Amnon was not necessarily a bad person. He actually thought he was truly in love. He was passionate about Tamar, he was confused about what to do, he wasn't eating, he told everyone that cared to ask how much he loved Tamar but after he slept with her, he also started asking himself what he was doing with her. By then he hated her even more than he loved her.

> *Then Amnon hated her with intense hatred. In fact, he hated her more than he had loved her. Amnon said to her, "Get up and get out!"*
>
> **—2 SAMUEL 13:15[NIV]**

This is what the average man says to you after he has slept with you. And even if he doesn't say it to you with his words or in his actions, he says it in his heart. You need to understand that sexual passion in men is way stronger than that of women. Women associate sex with love, men usually do not. A man can have sex with you and still not love you.

> *"No!" she said to him. "Sending me away would be a greater wrong than what you have already done to me." But he refused to listen to her. He called his personal servant and said, "Get this woman out of my sight and bolt the door after her."*
>
> **—2 SAMUEL 13:16-17[NIV]**

He hated her so much, he couldn't even stand her presence. He wanted her out of his sight and quickly too. He moved from what he thought was love to intense hatred all in one breath. So, to help you avoid such unpleasant experiences, I have written this book.

My passion in this is to help you clarify if what you are feeling is love and also to help you discover if what the person you love has for you is also love.

So, if you are ready, let's discover,

"… if he or she truly loves you."

SINGLE LADIES

If He Really
Loves You...

1

HE WILL PAY ATTENTION TO YOU

If a man truly loves you, he will pay attention to you. He will actually listen to you. In the narrative we read earlier, did you notice how many times the Bible mentioned that he refused to listen to her? It was mentioned significantly two times. And it's for a reason.

> But he <u>refused to listen to her,</u> and since he was stronger than she, he raped her.

> "No!" she said to him. "Sending me

away would be a greater wrong than what you have already done to me." But he <u>refused to listen to her.</u>

—2 SAMUEL 13:14 & 16[NIV]

Usually when a man loves you, he listens to you. So, if he can't pay attention to you, if he doesn't have time for you, if your opinion does not count regardless of what you say, then he doesn't love you. This is because, for men, attention is a very scarce commodity. Unlike women that can do more than one thing at the same time easily, men cannot. A man's attention is one of the ways you know what he values. So, if he is not paying attention to you, not listening to you, if he claims that he doesn't have time for you, then he doesn't love you.

The biggest lie men tell women they are

no longer interested in is, "I am busy." And that's it. The end. That is how to know that he has broken up with you. But most women, based on their nature, like closure. Women like to know precisely what's happening. So, you'll hear her say to the man, "Tell me exactly what you mean." As a marriage counsellor, permit me to tell you now, "The relationship is over." Don't wait for more heartbreak than that. Move on. You should also get busy with your life and trust God for a faithful man.

You need to understand this, when a man says he is busy, he is really busy. When he was chasing you all around, texting you every day, calling you every minute and taking you everywhere, that was work. He was busy working on you. And now that he has gotten what he wants from you, the contract has ended. He has moved on to another job. For most women this comes as a shock. They are wondering; how did he get to being busy all of a sudden? It's simple, he is either busy with something else or someone else... and the latter is usually the case.

So, attention is key! Ask yourself these questions...

- Does he pay attention to you?
- Does he listen to you?
- Can you actually get him to do things for you?
- Does he pay attention to what bothers you or what is important to you?

It was mentioned in the Scripture we read over and over again... *"he didn't listen to her."*

2

HE WILL BE WILLING TO WAIT FOR SEX

If he loves you, he will be willing to put sex aside to wait till there is the real commitment of marriage. A man that is impatient about waiting till marriage for sex usually is in love with sex and not you. When a man really loves you, he understands that this relationship is long-term, so sex will happen at the right time. But, when he has short term plans, he most likely has targeted how much he wants to invest and how far he would like to go with you. Therefore, trying to make him invest longer than he has planned is not a welcome idea. In his mind, he has two weeks planned out for the entire relationship, so when you tell him let's wait till marriage, he gets furious because you are messing up his plans.

I need you to know this, an impatient man usually doesn't love you because he has no long-term plans. If he loves you, and you tell him let's honour God by keeping ourselves pure sexually, he will appreciate that decision and begin to see you as someone precious. He knows that no matter how long it takes, you will still get married and he will then value you even more for waiting to have sex.

A man that doesn't love you can't wait. He will threaten you with, "If you don't have sex with me, I will be forced to have sex with other people." As silly as this sounds, some ladies will still remain in such relationships. If a man ever tells you this, know that what he loves is sex not you and that he has no respect for you. I have seen ladies in such situations come to me for counselling, asking what they should do. If someone has told you that if you don't have sex with him, that he will be free to go and have sex with whomever he wants, then he has shown you that you are nothing special to him, so believe him.

If a man really loves you, he will be okay with putting sex aside because he sees it as a long-term thing. Let's glean some more truths from Genesis 29:18-19[KJV],

> **And Jacob loved Rachel; and said, I will serve thee seven years for**

Rachel thy younger daughter. And Laban said, It is better that I give her to thee, than that I should give her to another man: abide with me.

Jacob was living with his uncle and he wanted to marry one of his uncle's daughters. A very pretty girl, but she was the younger daughter. He met his uncle and told him about his love for his daughter and that he would love to marry her. The bride price was set- seven years of hard labour and he was willing to pay the price because he loved her. So, he worked for seven years to marry her.

And Jacob served seven years for Rachel; and they seemed unto him but a few days, for the love he had to her. **—GENESIS 29:20[KJV]**

He didn't touch her through the seven years because he knew that at the end of the day, he would still get to marry her. He waited for seven years. So, when a man really loves you, he will be patient, he will be ready to wait till marriage to have sex with you.

The man that can't wait does not love you, it's sex he loves. Unfortunately, most ladies are so ignorant about this, they don't realize anybody sleeping with you before marriage will also have a problem staying faithful to you in marriage. Like I always say, every fornicator is an adulterer in training. Self-control doesn't end when you get married. You need self-control before and after you get married. God is trying to teach us something about discipline but many people are short circuiting the course, saying to themselves, let's just have sex it doesn't matter.

Most women honestly think that's how to keep a man faithful to them. But it doesn't work that way. If you engage in premarital sex, you are teaching the man that it is okay to take what is not legally his. You must understand that someone's intention to marry you is not the same thing as marriage. For instance, if you go to a shop and say you want to buy an item, that's just an offer, that's not an actual purchase until you pay. Can you imagine going to a car shop to say you want to buy a car, then you take the keys and drive it away without paying? It's when you buy it, that you can drive it away. But a lot of women miss it here. A man comes to you saying he wants to marry you; you respond with a "yes" and the next thing you do is take off your clothes. By the time you marry him, he will keep trying to take what is not legally his and by that time it won't be you, because by then you are his. He will keep trying to take other things because that is the training he has received from you. He has built an appetite for things that aren't his.

Most cases I have dealt with that involved adultery, 99.9% of them were cheating before they got married. Most women think once we are married, we will both stop cheating. It doesn't work that way with men. A man will continue cheating. So, if your relationship started with cheating, that is, both of you cheating on God by not keeping yourselves sexually pure, it will continue with him cheating on you and finally cheating will be the end of the relationship.

God has said sex should not come in till after marriage. He was very clear on that, but there are still couples planning to beat the system. Making clandestine moves God has specifically instructed them not to do. Now the question I have for you is, can two armed robbers keep to a pledge not to steal? Armed robbers don't trust anyone including themselves. So, in marriage, he is wondering, why do I have to stop cheating, is it because I am now married? Wedding vows cannot stop him. So, if he doesn't learn to have self-control now, he won't have it in marriage either. Marriage doesn't change anybody. A lizard that is single doesn't become an alligator in marriage. It's the same person.

So, going back to our story. Jacob worked for seven years and when he was done, a wedding date was fixed. On the wedding day, his bride was brought to him covered with a veil. He exchanged vows, married her and took her home. That was when he found out that he had been deceived, it was the older sister of the woman he loved that he had been given as a wife. And then, he went back to tell the family, there had been a mix up. That it was the younger daughter he wanted. That was when his father-in-law explained to him that based on their culture, the younger does not get married first. That's why he was given the older sister. Jacob insisted he wanted to marry the younger daughter still. So, his father-in-law told him he would need to serve another seven years for her, and he agreed.

> *... and he loved also Rachel more than Leah, and served with him yet seven other years.*
> **—GENESIS 29:30[KJV]**

Jacob worked for Laban for a total of fourteen years to marry Rachel. That's, in fact, how to know someone that's truly in love. A lot of ladies are in relationships with men that cannot wait for fourteen minutes, not to talk of fourteen days. Ladies, it is not you he loves, it is sex he loves and when he is done with you, he will move to another person. If he loves you, he will learn to put sex aside.

3

HE WILL BE GLAD AND QUICK TO INTRODUCE YOU TO THE PEOPLE THAT MATTER

If a man truly loves you, one of the things you will notice is that he is very proud of you and also quick to introduce you to the people that matter in his life. He might not post your picture on social media for people around the world to see or make a public announcement about you, because some men are private. However, he cannot be so private that nobody in this world knows that he is in a relationship with you. It's important you realize that if he claims to be so private that no one knows that he is in a relationship with you; he is most likely deceiving you. To think that a lot of ladies still fall for this kind of deception is so sad.

Marriage is not a private affair, in fact, it's quite the opposite. You can't marry undercover, so don't let anyone deceive you into a clandestine marriage. Marriage is a very public affair. When you get married, you will have children, will you hide them too? So even if he doesn't announce you publicly, the most important people in his life must know about you. But if he claims he has haters, at least his parents and pastors are not on the hater's list so he can introduce you to them. If he is hiding you from everybody, I have news for you, you are most likely not the only one he is dating. I have been a relationship coach for years and I keep teaching ladies these things, yet a lot of ladies still don't get it. I remember sometime ago, a lady came to me saying she was in a relationship with a particular young man. She said he was a celebrity and because of that he couldn't tell anyone about her. He also told her not to tell anyone about their relationship. So, no one was aware of this relationship. I tried to make her see that he was deceiving her, but she wouldn't believe me. A while later, she came back saying that he had broken up with her. I told her I wasn't surprised because he was never dating her, she was dating herself.

If a man is hiding you from the important

people in his life- his parents, his pastors, his boss, his mentors- he is deceiving you. Introducing you to his friends may mean nothing because they might all be in on it; they might all be deceiving you and using you. They may all know that you are not the one but will continue deceiving you, calling you "our wife." And when you visit your fiancé, they will ask you what you are cooking "for them". All they are after is what they will eat. In fact, his friends know the other girls he is dating and they are all consistently having meetings to know which girl is scoring points and which they will approve of for their friend.

So, if he is hiding you, let me just give it to you straight, he is scamming you. If he truly loves you, he will be glad to introduce you to the important people in his life. When I started dating my wife, the first thing I did was take her to my mentors. I introduced her to them and told her to feel free to call them if there were ever any issues.

4

HE WILL BE PROTECTIVE OF YOU

When a man really loves you, one of the things you will notice is that he will be very protective of you. This means that he will not put you through any form of abuse and he will be very protective of your welfare. Any man that is constantly verbally or emotionally abusing you now that he is still dating you, will most likely physically abuse you in marriage. Any man constantly threatening you, doesn't love you. If he loves you, he will protect you from everything and everyone possible including his own parents, siblings and family members. He won't throw you in their midst like a lamb amongst wolves. He won't allow his parents or siblings to terrorize you.

At different times in my marriage, I have had to protect my wife. In fact, before we got married, I remember the first time she came to visit me at home; my mother came in and met us talking in the parlour, she passed by and later came back in and asked my wife, "Is your mother not at home?" You might not understand what this means as a millennial or if you are from a younger generation but most older people will. It is a rhetorical question. When the mother of the man you are dating is asking you about your mother whom she is not acquainted with, what she is really saying is, "Don't you have anything to do at home? Go home and help your mother." I was very upset. When I got back home from seeing my wife off to the bus stop, I had a long conversation with my mother and I made sure she knew never to do it again.

You need to understand that your parents sometimes are emotionally bonded to you, so they become emotionally territorial around you. They don't mean harm most times, it's just that they are dealing with separation anxiety. This can be difficult especially for parents who have invested several years of their lives into raising you and being a part of your life. Most parents cannot stand the idea that someone they probably don't know too well just shows up and is about to take you away or replace them in your life. I have children as well, even though they are still very young, the thought of them leaving home for marriage still crosses my mind and it's not easy. The thought that a time will come when these children will be grown, have their own friends, have their phones, have their own lives, the very thought of it can cause anxiety for most parents so they react by becoming overly protective. They unconsciously start defending their territory emotionally. For some mothers, no matter the woman her son brings, she will think she is not good enough for him. But if a man really loves you, one of the things he must be willing to do is to protect you. He must be able to tell his parents that this is the person I want to marry; you are not at liberty to harass her. I had to have that serious talk with my mum and I did it because I love my wife.

Even when we got married it took us about eight years to have our first biological child. In the course of the eight years, no one had the liberty to come into our home to harass my wife as is common with African culture. In some families, sadly, if there is even a two years delay in childbirth, the mother-in-law, sisters-in-law, aunties will all move into the home and start harassing the wife. Those things should never happen if the man knows his place and loves his wife. Whenever there is a bullet to be shot by his family members, he should stand in for you because they can't shoot their own. Don't follow a man that will push you to them saying, "Go and do whatever mama says." If your mother is always calling to harass your fiancé or wife, as the man pick the phone and ask her how you may help her. And be sure to use a serious tone so she knows it's serious business.

Listen, if he loves you, he will protect you. He won't be the one pulling down your self-esteem, verbally insulting you or physically abusing you. If a man is doing these things to you and you are still asking if you should remain in such a relationship or what you should do, then there's a big problem. If he is slapping you when you are just dating then he will kill you in marriage because in marriage what we call, "over familiarity" steps in and he will most likely be tired of you by then. He should be taking care of you, not hurting you.

5

HE WILL INCLUDE YOU IN HIS FUTURE PLANS

If you want to know if he loves you, listen carefully to him whenever he is talking about his future. If he is using the word "I" instead of "We", you are not in the plans he has for his future. If you are having a conversation and he is saying things like, "I will like to live in Lagos" and you are supposed to be a couple and he is not saying, "We will live in Lagos" it means you are not in the future he is planning. If he says, "I would like my children to attend so or so school" instead of "our" children, it means you are not the mother of the children he is talking about just in case you don't know.

So, the question is, does he include you in his future plans? Listen closely, find out if he is including you in his future plans because men are very forward oriented, very future minded. If he is not including you in his future plans or sharing his future plans with you then you are not a part of that future because men are quick to share their future plans with the people they love. I have seen couples dating and the man puts together his documents and travels abroad while the lady has no clue. It's when he arrives there, he puts a call through to her to say he is in Canada. And the lady will call me to ask what to do. Usually, I tell such ladies that if he can plan to travel and his entire family was a part of it and none of them told you, it means that they have all agreed you are not the one. Simple.

6

HE WILL BE WILLING TO INVEST IN THE HEALTH OF YOUR RELATIONSHIP

If a man truly loves you, one of the things you will notice is that he will be willing to invest in the health and well-being of your relationship. He will make the necessary investments. He will be okay going with you for seminars that will help strengthen your relationship. He will spend time learning how to be better as an individual and how you can work better together as a couple.

This would be a major indication of love because the average man would rather go for financial training and work seminars. But if a man loves you, he will be open to going for marriage seminars or relationship counselling. He will start reading books on relationships just to promote the health of your own relationship.

Most men are not naturally relational. What this means is, they naturally won't prioritize things that focus on relationships, marital counselling, etc. However, when a man sees a lady he loves, he is usually willing to put in the necessary investment in order to get her. He will do whatever it takes to make her happy and keep her happy even if it means doing something out of the ordinary or something he doesn't even like to do.

SINGLE MEN AND WOMEN

If HE Or SHE
Loves You...

7

THEY WILL BE WILLING TO MAKE SACRIFICES FOR YOU

Anybody that cannot stress themselves for you doesn't love you. The Bible says, "For God so loved the world that He <u>gave</u>..." (John 3:16) And notice, He didn't just give anything He could find, He gave the most precious thing that He had- His <u>only</u> begotten son.

Sacrifice is another name for Love. If someone loves you, they will be willing to make sacrifices for you. They will sacrifice their money; they will sacrifice their time. Anybody that says they don't have time to call you is lying, he or she doesn't love you. Presidents have families and even in their busy schedule they still keep in touch with whom they want to keep in touch with.

When you see a man that is in love, nowhere is too far. If he lives in Lagos and his fiancé lives in Benin City, he will tell his colleagues and friends, "Guys on Friday, I will close from work early, I need to get somewhere" When asked where, he'd say, "Benin City" (A state in Nigeria) When his friends exclaim at the distance, he'd tell them, "Is it not just Benin City here? It's not far." (Benin City is 200 miles from Lagos State). Nowhere is too far for someone in Love because the object of his love is there. However, if he is not trained, after he marries you even the next room is too far. If you ask him for a favour, he will say, "No, I can't stand up, it's too far"

If he loves you, he will gladly spend his money sacrificially on you. Any man that cannot spend his money on you is stingy and loves money, he doesn't love you.

The same thing goes with when a woman loves you, she will be willing to spend her money, help you and give you material things without you asking, once she perceives you need it. She can't hear that you have need of something that she has and won't release it for your use and even if she doesn't have it, she will be willing to find a way to get it for you. for instance, if your laptop battery suddenly develops a fault, she can sacrifice her own laptop for you to use. If she loves you, she will willingly give to you.

So, sacrifice is the name of the game.

CONCLUSION

God is very much interested in love and marriages. This might come as a shock to a lot of people especially in these times, but the truth remains- He still is. Love is His very nature. And contrary to what many people think, Love is first a spiritual virtue. A relationship with God is very crucial to walking in love. If you are not born again you can't walk in the God kind of love which is the love that truly sustains all blissful relationships and marriages.

So, if you are yet to give your heart to Christ, this is a good opportunity to do so. God reserves good and perfect gifts for His children. Come into God's fold today. And because He is Love, let Him help you become the kind of person you should be and also find the kind of love that you should have. It's really simple. Just say this prayer from your heart:

Lord Jesus, I come to you today. I acknowledge that I am a sinner and I believe you came, died and rose again to save me. I open my heart to you and confess with my mouth that you are my Lord

and Saviour from today onwards. [Romans 10:9-10]. Thank You Lord for saving and transforming me. Now, I am born-again

and I know that my life will never be the same. I receive the grace to serve you all the days of my life.

OTHER BOOKS BY KINGSLEY & MILDRED OKONKWO

- When Am I Ready?
- Who Should I Marry?
- 25 Wrong Reasons People Enter Relationships.
- Just Us Girls
- I Love You But My Parents Say No
- Should Ladies Propose?
- God Told Me To Marry You
- Waiting For Isaac
- 7 Questions Wise Women Ask
- 7 Qualities Wise Men Want
- Chayil- The Virtuous Woman
- A-Z Of Marriage
- Help! My Husband Is Acting Funny
- All Year Round- For Men
- All Year Round- For Women
- Chayil Prayer Journal
- Hannah's Heart Devotional
- Manual- The Way Men think
- Simply Attractive. (e-book)
- 21 Days Sexual Purity Devotional (e-book)
- 21 Days Prayers and Fasting For Expectant Mothers. (e-book)
- One Thing
- God Can Be Trusted- Volume 1 & 2
- How to Know If He or She Really Loves You
- 7 Things I Badly Want To Tell Women (New Book)

HOW TO KNOW IF **SHE** REALLY LOVES YOU

KINGSLEY OKONKWO

CONTENTS

DEDICATION

To all the men who desire to understand the true meaning of love as well as avoid unpleasant experiences so that they can be better guided in the choice of a life partner and ultimately have the marriage of their dreams.

INTRODUCTION

No one wants to spend their lives with someone who doesn't love them. And this makes absolute sense. Why on earth would you want to be in a relationship with or plan to get married to someone who you are not absolutely sure you love or loves you in return? Love is the very essence of relationships and marriages. As a matter of fact, one of the most common questions I get asked during counselling sessions is, "Pastor, how do I know if a person truly loves me?" And it is so important to ask this question because a lot of single people actually think what they have for each other is love. Love, unfortunately, is one of the most misunderstood, misconstrued and misrepresented words in our world today.

In a relationship, it is easy to hear people say, "I love you." But after they get married, they realize they never truly loved each other. Every couple that is divorced today thought at some point that they loved their spouse. At some point they felt, "I love this man or woman" but later, it became, "I hate this man or woman." So, you actually need to be able to know if what you are feeling is love because not every feeling you have is love. A lot of single people are not so knowledgeable in this regard, so they assume every feeling they have is love.

A young lady might meet a nice-looking man for the first time and because she loses her composure around him and can't seem to forget him, she assumes it is love. No, that's not love. You need to understand that there are many other emotions that feel or look like love but they are not love. Just because you are always thinking about a man or woman does not mean you love them. In fact, some of those feelings are just infatuation or obsession or sexual attraction. You will eventually have such feelings for many other people as you go through life but it is not necessarily always love.

2 Samuel 13:1-17(NIV) tells a very remarkable story to buttress this;

> *In the course of time, Amnon son of David fell in love with Tamar, the beautiful sister of Absalom son of David.*

Amnon became so obsessed with his sister Tamar that he made himself ill. She was a virgin, and it seemed impossible for him to do anything to her.

In our time, we would say, no doubt what Amnon had for Tamar was true love. He couldn't eat, he was growing thin, in fact he was sick; love sick. I also see single people go through the same thing these days. You'll hear them say things like, "When I see him or her, I can't breathe..." Immediately, I tell them, "That's not love, that is an asthma attack, go and get an inhaler."

Amnon, also, was so obsessed with his half-sister Tamar, that he made himself sick. Let's read on,

Now Amnon had an adviser named Jonadab son of Shimeah, David's

brother. Jonadab was a very shrewd man.

Please note this, one of the biggest lessons you can learn from this is that as a single person, you cannot successfully fail without bad friends or bad advice. That is why getting the right knowledge about relationships and surrounding yourself with the right people is key.

He asked Amnon, "Why do you, the king's son, look so haggard morning after morning? Won't you tell me?" Amnon said to him, "I'm in love with Tamar, my brother Absalom's sister."

"Go to bed and pretend to be ill," Jonadab said. "When your father comes to see you, say to him, 'I would like my sister Tamar to come and give me something to eat. Let

her prepare the food in my sight so I may watch her and then eat it from her hand.'"

So Amnon lay down and pretended to be ill. When the king came to see him, Amnon said to him, "I would like my sister Tamar to come and make some special bread in my sight, so I may eat from her hand."

David sent word to Tamar at the palace: "Go to the house of your brother Amnon and prepare some food for him." So Tamar went to the house of her brother Amnon, who was lying down. She took some dough, kneaded it, made the bread in his sight and baked it. Then she took the pan and served him the bread, but he refused to eat.

"Send everyone out of here," Amnon said. So everyone left him. Then

Amnon said to Tamar, "Bring the food here into my bedroom so I may eat from your hand." And Tamar took the bread she had prepared and brought it to her brother Amnon in his bedroom. But when she took it to him to eat, he grabbed her and said, "Come to bed with me, my sister."

"No, my brother!" she said to him. "Don't force me! Such a thing should not be done in Israel! Don't do this wicked thing. What about me? Where could I get rid of my disgrace? And what about you? You would be like one of the wicked fools in Israel. Please speak to the king; he will not keep me from being married to you." But he refused to listen to her, and since he was stronger than she, he raped her.

Then Amnon hated her with intense

hatred. In fact, he hated her more than he had loved her. Amnon said to her, "Get up and get out!"

This is such a sad story because this is still the reality for some people, even today, which is why I believe everyone must learn about relationships. Take a closer look at what happened here. Prior to this, Amnon thought he was in love with Tamar; he couldn't eat, couldn't sleep, he was sick and everyone around saw how much it was affecting him too. It wasn't a prank, he wasn't faking it, but the problem was not love, maybe infatuation, maybe lust, maybe just sexual passion but it was definitely not love. So, if you notice, once he got what he wanted everything changed. Single ladies you can take a lesson from this, you need to understand this, when a man sleeps with you, the way he sees you changes. Before he sleeps with you, he feels like he can't live without you, he's thinking of you constantly, he's calling you every time but once he sleeps with you everything changes. He also can't explain what is happening; he doesn't understand why all of a sudden, he can't stand you, he cannot place his fingers on why he hates you so much, but he just does. Sadly, some people experience this shift in marriage.

A lot of people, like Amnon, also think what they have for one another is love and because of this they rush into marriage only to discover it has nothing to do with love but by that time, they are already married with children. And that is why God tells single people to keep sex out of their relationships. Sex confuses issues and that's the problem. So, keeping sex out of your relationship is one of the quickest ways to know the person that truly loves you.

Amnon was not necessarily a bad person. He actually thought he was truly in love. He was passionate about Tamar, he was confused about what to do, he wasn't eating, he told everyone that cared to ask how much he loved Tamar but after he slept with her, he also started asking himself what he was doing with her. By then he hated her even more than he loved her.

> *Then Amnon hated her with intense hatred. In fact, he hated her more than he had loved her. Amnon said to her, "Get up and get out!"*
>
> **—2 SAMUEL 13:15[NIV]**

This is what the average man says to you after he has slept with you. And even if he doesn't say it to you with his words or in his actions, he says it in his heart. You need to understand that sexual passion in men is way stronger than that of women. Women associate sex with love, men usually do not. A man can have sex with you and still not love you.

> *"No!" she said to him. "Sending me away would be a greater wrong than what you have already done to me." But he refused to listen to her. He called his personal servant and said, "Get this woman out of my sight and bolt the door after her."*
>
> **—2 SAMUEL 13:16-17[NIV]**

He hated her so much, he couldn't even stand her presence. He wanted her out of his sight and quickly too. He moved from what he thought was love to intense hatred all in one breath. So, to help you avoid such unpleasant experiences, I have written this book.

My passion in this is to help you clarify if what you are feeling is love and also to help you discover if what the person you love has for you is also love.

So, if you are ready, let's discover,

"… if he or she truly loves you."

SINGLE MEN

If SHE Really Loves You...

1

SHE WILL BE COMMITTED TO YOU

If a woman loves you, she will be totally dedicated to you. She will be glad to post your picture everywhere, on her phone, on her social media platforms, she will be glad to talk about you, you won't feel emotionally distant from her or even feel like you don't have her full attention, you will be sure of her 100% commitment. Usually, women have the capacity to run more than one thing at the same time, but when she is in love with you, she shuts all others down for you. Most men don't know this but when a woman loves you, she will give you her undivided attention.

However, women have a common dilemma- most women have no choice but to wait till men approach them. On the other hand, men choose whoever they want to approach. So sometimes a man that a woman doesn't really like might come along and because she is not in any relationship yet she holds on to him first while hopeful that her tall, dark and handsome will still come. So, she is in one relationship but still entertaining several chats from some other prospective men. Most times when women cheat or double date, it is largely because they are not satisfied with who they are with. Men cheat for a different reason. A man can be with a woman he loves very much and still be tempted to cheat. Women are not like that, if a woman is really in love she has no time for any other person, she doesn't give any other person the time of day. There is nothing as horrible as wooing a woman in love, you are totally wasting your energy. She won't give you any iota of her time. If a woman is in a relationship and she is still entertaining other men, take it from me she is not happy with the person she is in a relationship with. She either doesn't think the man is her best option or she used to love the man and now the man is messing up big time and she is getting tired of him and looking for a backup plan. So, most times if you see a woman cheating, it's usually because she is not satisfied with the man she's with but a man on the other hand can be very satisfied with whom he has married but his roaming spirit is still making his eyes go everywhere. A lot of the men that cheat have great wives at home- women that are beautiful, can cook, take care of the home, etc. When a woman cheats, it's either her husband is cheating as well and she wants revenge or she married below her level because time was not on her side and she was desperate, and she is now aware that she should not have married him.

Women, interestingly, have the capacity to multi-date with ease. If a man is cheating, it is usually so obvious because all his attention will be on his new relationship and everyone will know that he has neglected his wife. This is because a man's attention is usually one-sided. If he wants to take his bath, he will hide his phone, his password will have a password, everyone will know he is hiding something. But, if a woman is trying to catch the attention of a man, no one will know. Women are very smart emotionally.

A lot of men actually feel they wooed a woman, not knowing the women are the ones that chose them. When a woman enters a room, she immediately scans the room and knows the men that are eligible and the ones that are not. She has seen the ones that have a chance with her and the ones that will never make it through to her. In fact, some women already have the answer that they will give you if you ever come to them someday saying you love them because she has seen the way you are looking at her, so she has prepared your "No" and is just waiting to serve you with it. If she spots the people she wants, no matter what she is doing, she will find a way to ensure their paths cross so that they will notice her; if they are seated in a particular area, she will come up with excuses to pass by them to get their attention. Then when she is eventually near the person she likes and he cracks a little joke, she will laugh so hard and so long while maximizing every opportunity to touch him flirtatiously. Women are so sleek and intentional about relationships. This, in fact, makes it easy to identify women who don't love their husbands, they hardly ever post his pictures online or talk about him, they will rather post pictures of their children or something else. When a married woman's husband is misbehaving, she will most times shift her attention to her children. However, this only applies to the good wives because the bad ones will simply shift it to another man.

If a woman is cheating, her other relationships will still be fine- every member of her family will still feel loved the normal way. She will still be diligent in her work, love her husband and children and love her boyfriend as well. If a man is cheating, everyone will feel neglected except the person he is cheating with. This is because men can't do more than one thing at a time.

So, if she loves you, she will close all other offers and focus on you. And you will know it because she will give you 100% dedication.

2

SHE WILL PRAY FOR YOU

A woman who loves you will pray for you. That's the truth. If a woman really loves you, especially if she is a spiritual woman it will come to her naturally to pray for you. When women love you, they pour out their hearts to God for you. It is a natural instinct. This doesn't mean men don't or shouldn't pray but because women are passionate lovers, they want you to become your best self and as such pray fervently for you and just like the Bible notes that the effectual, fervent prayer of the righteous man availeth much (James 5:16). You will see progress in your life.

If your father loves you, all he will most likely do is to advise you but when your mother loves you, she will pray for you. A lot of people are alive and thriving because they had praying mothers. A woman is passionate, and she channels her passion to prayers. Most women have no prayer points for themselves, they pray solely for their kids or spouses. So, when a woman loves you, she prays for you and there is nothing as powerful as that passionate prayer.

My wife prays for me passionately and that is one of the things that gives me strength. She also has a book on this, "Praying For Your Husband" where she lists out sample prayers she has prayed for me over the years. Whether you are married or not, if you like how my life is going then get it so you will know how to pray for your husband or your future husband as well.

3

SHE WANTS TO SAVE YOUR RESOURCES AND NOT SQUANDER IT

A woman who loves you will be interested in saving your resources and not squandering it. This is actually one of the ways you know a lady that is interested in your life. If she is looking for how to get from you, she really doesn't love you. Women are natural givers when they love you, they won't really be focused on taking from you instead they want to give to you. If all she is after is always how you will buy things for her or send her money, she doesn't love you. If all she wants is to keep spending your money, she doesn't love you. If you take her out, and she picks up the menu and orders everything on the menu without thinking about whether you can afford it or not then it's a sign that she doesn't love you. I say this because when a woman loves you, she would prefer to save your money and invest it towards your future together. She will prefer to cook rather than eat out if that will help you save money. Her focus will be on saving your resources not on squandering them.

Sometimes, during the preparation phase for a couples traditional wedding in Nigeria, after the man has been given an outrageous bride price list and his bride-to-be sees the list, she will tell her husband-to-be to go and get the money in whatever way he can, that's how it's done in her culture knowing fully well that there's no way he can afford such an exorbitant list. Any woman that does that doesn't love you because if she loves you, she will go to her parents and appeal to them saying where is he going to get such money from that he is a young man just starting life. She will plead that the list be reduced, and unnecessary things be struck off the list.

I remember when I was about getting married, my father-in-law told me to move the date because they had just done a wedding and couldn't support us financially if we wanted to get married that year and they really wanted to. I boldly told him we didn't need any support, I asked for the list saying I wanted to get married that year. When the list was given to me, by the way, any list with regards to marriage that comes directly from the village will have no decency and conscience. The list was three foolscap sheets. When I looked at the list, I was sad, embarrassed, confused, I went through different phases of emotions all at once. I had to mask it all with a smile even though I was crying on the inside. I didn't know what to say or how to react. I couldn't afford all that was on the list. And thank God my wife went to her parents and pleaded that I was a young pastor and couldn't afford all the items on the list. Even some of the things on the list that were not taken out, like a box of clothes, she sorted all that out on her own. My wife was such a major blessing during our wedding, so today that I can afford to buy her almost anything she wants. I don't hesitate to because she has always been interested in saving for me. So, when she loves you, she won't want to stress you.

If she is the one insisting that you must get all the items on the list, then she doesn't love you. These days we have a lot of women who should be married still living in their parents houses because their parents are dishing out unreasonable bridal lists to prospective suitors. The economy has changed, things are more expensive now than when those lists were written. If she is more interested in you spending all you have to throw a big wedding just to make a statement, it's not you she loves. If she loves you, she will save your resources and not squander them.

4

SHE WILL BE INCREDIBLY TOLERANT AND FORGIVING OF YOU

If a woman loves you, there is nothing you can do to offend her that she won't forgive. Meanwhile, if she hates you, there is nothing you can do that will make her happy. In fact, if a woman is angry with you, even if you kill yourself to make her happy, she will still complain saying, "Is that how your mates die?" But if she loves you, there is nothing you can do that she can't forgive. When she loves you, she may even seem to be living in denial. I have seen some women live like this, the man is doing absolutely crazy things, and everyone around can see it that he is unwise, but she refuses to admit it saying there's wisdom in what he is doing. She sees only the best in him.

A lot of women have married armed robbers and fraudsters- people who are notorious and not good for them. These women will even cover their spouses. Women in love will go to any length for you, so if you are dating someone and any little issue, she tells you she can't take it and you break up every week then she doesn't love you. When a woman loves you, one of the ways to know is that she will be incredibly tolerant and forgiving of you. Sometimes, you may even feel like what you've done is unforgivable, but she will keep seeing the best in you and will stick around till you change.

5

SHE WILL KNOW YOUR DREAMS AND WILL BE COMMITTED TO BRINGING THEM TO PASS

Women are natural incubators. That's why they have wombs. God had a reason He gave men the seed and women the womb. And it is simple. A woman naturally wants to nurture and birth things. It is instinctive for her to birth. That's why, when a woman is married, she feels bad when she doesn't have children. She is seeing that she has a womb and God has also given her breasts; both are to incubate and nurture. So, birthing instinctively comes with her territory.

When you enter a woman's life, she is looking at how she can receive the seed of your dream, nurture it, birth it and bring it back to you. If she loves you, she will be interested in your dreams. Most men are in relationships with women who have no idea of what they do for a living, Women who don't know their dreams. When you marry the right woman, she will see to it that your dreams come to pass. There's nothing like a woman that is committed to a man's dream.

One of the things God will give to you when He is happy with you is a good wife. If you marry a good woman and you treat her well, there is nothing you want to achieve that she won't make happen. She will make sure you maximize your potential. There was a woman like that in the Bible. She was a bad woman but a good wife.

Let's read 1st Kings 21:4[NIV]

> *Some time later there was an incident involving a vineyard belonging to Naboth the Jezreelite. The vineyard was in Jezreel, close to the palace of Ahab king of Samaria. Ahab said to Naboth, "Let me have your vineyard to use for a vegetable garden, since it is close to my palace. In exchange I will give you a better vineyard or, if you prefer, I will pay you whatever it is worth."*
>
> *But Naboth replied, "The LORD forbid*

that I should give you the inheritance of my ancestors."

So Ahab went home, sullen and angry because Naboth the Jezreelite had said, "I will not give you the inheritance of my ancestors." He lay on his bed sulking and refused to eat.

His wife Jezebel came in and asked him, "Why are you so sullen? Why won't you eat?"

He answered her, "Because I said to Naboth the Jezreelite, 'Sell me your vineyard; or if you prefer, I will give you another vineyard in its place.' But he said, 'I will not give you my vineyard.'"

Jezebel his wife said, "Is this how you act as king over Israel? Get up and eat! Cheer up. I'll get you the vineyard of Naboth the Jezreelite."

Jezebel was no doubt a bad woman,

but she was a good wife. The story we read above shows us how her husband wanted to fulfill his dream, but he was denied the privilege and because of this, he went back home sulking. Jezebel noticed his countenance and asked why he was so sad and not eating. After he told her the reason, she told him to cheer up and eat, that she would get him the vineyard. This happens all the time in my house. Once my wife notices that my countenance is down, she will come asking what's wrong. And after I tell her, she will tell me not to worry that it's done. She will pick her phone and sort it out. She will handle the issue seamlessly.

Every man needs a woman like this. Unfortunately, some women don't know when their husband's countenance is down. They don't even know their husband's dream, so how will they know when it comes to pass or how will they know what to pray about?

Most men are better at dreaming while women are better with details. And this can be seen from the story above. Ahab had the dream, but the acquisition detail was sorted out by Jezebel. She handled 'the how'; called the elders, got people to accuse Naboth, killed him and confiscated the land for her husband. That was it.

So, when she loves you, she will know your dreams and will be very committed to it.

6

SHE ALWAYS WANTS TO BE WITH YOU AND BE IN TOUCH WITH YOU

Women talk for affection; men talk for information. A man doesn't call you unless he has something important to tell you but women on the other hand talk to you because they love you, they don't need to have something to tell you. They talk for affection. If a man is calling, he is not just calling, he is doing so to ask you for something or tell you something important. If a woman is calling you, most times she doesn't necessarily have anything to tell you, she just wants to know how you are doing. Men on the other hand always have a reason when they call and that's why a woman gets so upset when she is in a relationship and her fiancé does not keep in touch or call to know how she is doing. If you are married and both of you left home together that morning, by noon it's important to call her to still check up on her. In the world of women that makes perfect sense. Because women love to keep in touch. Men on the other hand are not like that. If a man tells another man that he is going home, that is it. They won't call each other to find out if they have gotten home or not, it is not necessary but if a woman tells you she is going home, you need to call to find out if she is home.

Most men that use women leverage on that greatly, they only keep in touch with such women when they want to sleep with them and quite sadly most women still fall for such tactics. When a woman loves you, she wants your attention, she wants to hear from you and talk to you. If she isn't eager to talk to you or spend time with you, she probably doesn't love you.

SINGLE MEN AND WOMEN

If HE Or SHE
Loves You...

7

THEY WILL BE WILLING TO MAKE SACRIFICES FOR YOU

Anybody that cannot stress themselves for you doesn't love you. The Bible says, "For God so loved the world that He <u>gave</u>..." (John 3:16) And notice, He didn't just give anything He could find, He gave the most precious thing that He had- His <u>only</u> begotten son.

Sacrifice is another name for Love. If someone loves you, they will be willing to make sacrifices for you. They will sacrifice their money; they will sacrifice their time. Anybody that says they don't have time to call you is lying, he or she doesn't love you. Presidents have families and even in their busy schedule they still keep in touch with whom they want to keep in touch with.

When you see a man that is in love, nowhere is too far. If he lives in Lagos and his fiancé lives in Benin City, he will tell his colleagues and friends, "Guys on Friday, I will close from work early, I need to get somewhere" When asked where, he'd say, "Benin City" (A state in Nigeria) When his friends exclaim at the distance, he'd tell them, "Is it not just Benin City here? It's not far." (Benin City is 200 miles from Lagos State). Nowhere is too far for someone in Love because the object of his love is there. However, if he is not trained, after he marries you even the next room is too far. If you ask him for a favour, he will say, "No, I can't stand up, it's too far"

If he loves you, he will gladly spend his money sacrificially on you. Any man that cannot spend his money on you is stingy and loves money, he doesn't love you.

The same thing goes with when a woman loves you, she will be willing to spend her money, help you and give you material things without you asking, once she perceives you need it. She can't hear that you have need of something that she has and won't release it for your use and even if she doesn't have it, she will be willing to find a way to get it for you. for instance, if your laptop battery suddenly develops a fault, she can sacrifice her own laptop for you to use. If she loves you, she will willingly give to you.

So, sacrifice is the name of the game.

CONCLUSION

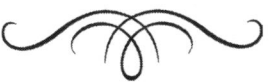

God is very much interested in love and marriages. This might come as a shock to a lot of people especially in these times, but the truth remains- He still is. Love is His very nature. And contrary to what many people think, Love is first a spiritual virtue. A relationship with God is very crucial to walking in love. If you are not born again you can't walk in the God kind of love which is the love that truly sustains all blissful relationships and marriages.

So, if you are yet to give your heart to Christ, this is a good opportunity to do so. God reserves good and perfect gifts for His children. Come into God's fold today. And because He is Love, let Him help you become the kind of person you should be and also find the kind of love that you should have. It's really simple. Just say this prayer from your heart:

Lord Jesus, I come to you today. I acknowledge that I am a sinner and I believe you came, died and rose again to save me. I open my heart to you and confess with my mouth that you are my Lord

and Saviour from today onwards. [Romans 10:9-10]. Thank You Lord for saving and transforming me. Now, I am born-again

and I know that my life will never be the same. I receive the grace to serve you all the days of my life.

OTHER BOOKS BY KINGSLEY & MILDRED OKONKWO

- When Am I Ready?
- Who Should I Marry?
- 25 Wrong Reasons People Enter Relationships.
- Just Us Girls
- I Love You But My Parents Say No
- Should Ladies Propose?
- God Told Me To Marry You
- Waiting For Isaac
- 7 Questions Wise Women Ask
- 7 Qualities Wise Men Want
- Chayil- The Virtuous Woman
- A-Z Of Marriage
- Help! My Husband Is Acting Funny
- All Year Round- For Men
- All Year Round- For Women
- Chayil Prayer Journal
- Hannah's Heart Devotional
- Manual- The Way Men think
- Simply Attractive. (e-book)
- 21 Days Sexual Purity Devotional (e-book)
- 21 Days Prayers and Fasting For Expectant Mothers. (e-book)
- One Thing
- God Can Be Trusted- Volume 1 & 2
- How to Know If He or She Really Loves You
- 7 Things I Badly Want To Tell Women (New Book)

Made in the USA
Columbia, SC
19 August 2024